D0327574

you're not a kid anymore when . . .

Jeff Foxworthy

Illustrations by David Boyd

LONGSTREET PRESS
Atlanta, Georgia

Published by LONGSTREET PRESS, INC.,
a subsidiary of Cox Newspapers,
a division of Cox Enterprises, Inc.
2140 Newmarket Parkway
Suite 122
Marietta, Georgia 30067

Printed in the United States of America

11th printing, 1997

Library of Congress Catalog Number 93-79656

ISBN: 1-56352-102-4

This book was printed by Data Reproductions Corporation, Rochester Hills, Michigan.
The text was set in New Baskerville

Cover design by Graham & Co. Graphics
Book design by Jill Dible

To my Mom and Dad . . .
Now I understand and appreciate your wisdom and experience.

Also by Jeff Foxworthy

You Might Be A Redneck If . . .
Hick Is Chic
Red Ain't Dead
Check Your Neck

Jeff Foxworthy is also available on CD and cassette by Warner Bros.

Foreword

A popular soap opera begins, "Like sand through the hour glass, so are the days of our lives." No doubt true, and a little disturbing when you realize the bottom half of your own personal hour-glass is starting to resemble the Sahara desert. Let's face it: your sweet bird of youth has flown the coup and she ain't coming back.

How did this happen? Where did the years go? The irony of it all hit me not long ago, as my wife and I and several friends were looking through old photo albums. We came across some photos of yours truly decked out in my hottest disco threads (skin-tight, shiny copper pants and a cream colored silk shirt . . . John Travolta, eat your heart out). Well, the rest of the group was laughing so hard the dryness of their underwear was in serious jeopardy. I just sat there thinking, "#*@!, that was probably the coolest I'll ever be in my life! Cool, not funny."

What happened? I do know that at one point in my life I was hip. I was! I knew all the right bands, the great songs, the right clothes, and the right expressions. My parents hated my hair! There was no such thing as music that was too loud. No sleep? Who cared? Sleep was for people with no life . . . or was it?

I certainly feel like I have a life. I am a husband, a father, and an assortment of other things designed to make enough money to continue being a husband

and a father (wives and children are big-ticket items). I work harder and sleep less than I ever have in the past. I also find myself doing things I swore I would never do. One evening not long ago while watering the lawn, I yelled at someone for driving down our street too fast. As soon as I realized what I had done, I dropped the hose and began to shake. I am becoming my dad! I'm getting old.

If you found the title of this book interesting enough to pick it up and you're reading this, you have no doubt secretly, or not too secretly, found yourself in the same boat. Maybe even seated next to people with whom you swore you would never have anything in common.

What do we do? Schedule emergency liposuction? Get fitted for a toupe? You could. You could also go broke trying to be the person you once were. It's not worth it. You didn't like yourself that much then anyway, and your kids are looking forward to the inheritance. Or . . . you could just accept it, which is probably the best thing to do.

Solving the world's problems is a young man's or woman's game. Revolution requires a lot of energy. Enjoy the changes that each new chapter in life brings. Accept that which you cannot change. Love yourself for who you are now. And above all else, remember this . . . The mirror is no longer your friend.

Age Gracefully,
Jeff Foxworthy

You're not a kid anymore when . . .

You're asleep, but others worry that you're dead.

You find yourself admiring a pair
of pants at Sears.

. . .

Your back goes out more than you do.

. . .

You no longer laugh at Preparation H
commercials.

You can live
without sex but
not without
your glasses.

You buy shoes with crepe rubber soles.

• • •

You quit trying to hold in your stomach, no matter who walks into the room.

• • •

The family Christmas party is held at your house.

Your arms are almost too short to read the newspaper.

You're not a kid anymore when . . .

You use the phrase "new-fangled" in
a sentence.

. . .

You have to reintroduce yourself at your class
reunion . . . and you were class president.

. . .

You buy a compass for the dash of your car.

The only reason you're still awake at
4 A.M. is indigestion.

The pharmacy gives you a volume discount.

• • •

People ask what color your hair used to be.

• • •

You are proud of your lawnmower.

Your best friend is dating someone half his age . . . and isn't breaking any laws.

You can't sleep if the house is a mess.

• • •

You call Olan Mills before they call you.

• • •

You give up hoping you'll get carded at
the liquor store.

You start singing along with the elevator music.

You constantly talk about the price of gasoline.

· · ·

You really do want a new washing machine
for your birthday.

· · ·

An old lady offers you her seat on the bus.

Your car must have four doors.

• • •

You enjoy watching the news.

• • •

You would rather go to work than
stay home sick.

You make an appointment to see the dentist.

• • •

The phone rings and you hope it's not for you.

• • •

You routinely check the oil in your car.

14

You've owned clothes so long that they've come back into style . . . twice.

You no longer think of speed limits
as a challenge.

• • •

You realize you've been sitting at the "big table"
for Thanksgiving dinner longer than
you can remember.

• • •

You worry whether you have
enough insurance.

You consider
coffee one of the
most important
things in life.

You're not a kid anymore when . . .

You write "thank-you" notes without being told.

• • •

You don't remember when you got that
mole . . . or the one next to it . . . .

• • •

8 A.M. is your idea of "sleeping in."

You enjoy hearing about other people's operations.

19

Neighbors borrow your tools.

• • •

Your biggest concern when dancing is falling.

• • •

You have a dream about prunes.

People call you at
at 9 P.M. and ask,
"Did I wake you?"

You can't climb a tree . . . even with a ladder.

• • •

You've recently said, "I can't hear myself think!"

• • •

You forget your own birthday.

Your bathing suit
has sleeves.

You browse in the bran cereal section
of the grocery store.

• • •

You answer a question with,
"Because I said so!"

• • •

You start worrying when your supply of
Ben-Gay is low.

You tell the barber
to comb it over the
best he can.

Others ask for your recipes.

• • •

You play golf with your wife.

• • •

You yell at the paperboy for damaging
your flower beds.

You've worn out the T.V. Guide by Thursday.

• • •

You start Christmas shopping in August.

• • •

You send money to PBS.

You still buy records.

• • •

You no longer answer, "Fine," when people ask how you are.

• • •

The bank sends you a birthday card.

You no longer run up stairs.

You paint the walls for a reason other than getting your deposit back.

• • •

You think a C.D. is a certificate of deposit.

• • •

You need a new apron.

The end of your tie doesn't come anywhere near the top of your pants.

DAVID BOYD

Your name is on a waiting list at the library.

• • •

Sons and daughters of relatives you barely
remember send you graduation
and wedding invitations.

• • •

You don't like to drive after dark.

You stop watering the lawn to yell at someone for driving too fast down your street.

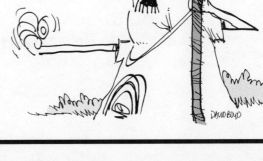

DAVID BOYD

Your high school diploma is
the color of buttermilk.

. . .

You tell people to call you collect.

. . .

Things you bought new start showing up
in antique stores.

Your Chihuahua weighs more than 25 pounds.

DAVID BOYD

You start defending one-piece bathing suits.

• • •

You seriously consider a burial plot.

• • •

You take a metal detector to the beach.

You have more than two spare pair of glasses.

DAVID BOYD

You read the obituaries daily.

• • •

You have your own lawyer.

• • •

You say the words, "Turn that music down!"

Digestion is a consideration when reading a menu.

WHAT DO YOU HAVE THAT'S BEEN ORDERED TWICE BY A PERSON MY AGE?

Tony's

DAVID BOYD

People call you to get someone's address.

• • •

You will not go downtown alone.

• • •

You begin a sentence by saying,
"When I was your age...."

You wear black socks with sandals.

DAVID BOYD

You point out what buildings used to be where.

• • •

You give your used furniture to other people . . . and they're happy to get it.

• • •

You know which one is the soup spoon, and you use it.

You know all the warning signs of a heart attack.

You rake the yard without being made to.

• • •

When you sit down, someone brings you
a lap blanket.

• • •

You know what the word "equity" means.

You are alarmed
by how young
your doctor is.

AAA makes good sense.

• • •

College students call you "ma'am" or "sir."

• • •

You'd rather have a new dishwasher
than a new stereo.

You tie ties for other people.

You "Shuuusssh" people during a movie.

• • •

Nobody ever tells you to "Slow down!"

• • •

You fill up the tank whenever you buy gas.

You win a "Yard of the Month" award.

You're not a kid anymore when . . .

You left the last concert you attended because
you had a headache.

• • •

You wear pearls with everything.

• • •

You can't remember the last time you lay on
the floor to watch television.

You're thinking about giving up belts
for suspenders.

● ● ●

Your hair brush hurts your scalp.

● ● ●

You listen to only "talk radio."

You realize you're not going to win the lottery.

. . .

Your eyebrows look like shrubbery and your wife's have disappeared.

. . .

The service station attendant lets you pump your gas before paying.

You can't remember the last time someone told you to get a haircut.

53

You make everyone be quiet during
weather bulletins.

. . .

You worry less about breaking the law and
more about breaking a hip.

. . .

You have time to write a letter . . . every day.

You name your hot water bottle.

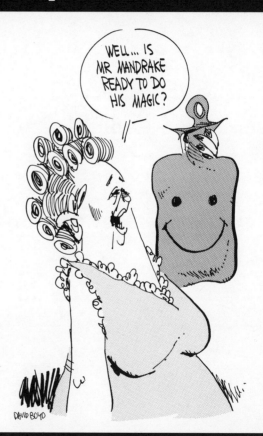

You have a party and the neighbors
don't even realize it.

• • •

You can quickly find anything in your garage.

• • •

It takes two hands to hold up your underwear.

Your bell-bottoms are belled at both ends.

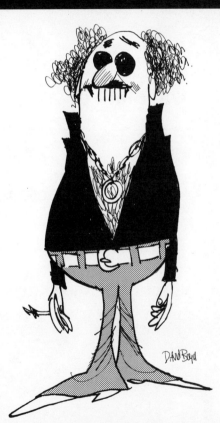

You don't own a pair of tennis shoes.

• • •

All your pants are dress pants.

• • •

You can't make any article of clothing
look provocative.

You have to get a permit to light the candles on your birthday cake.

You think about Walter Cronkite at least
once a day.

• • •

You drive the interstate and never leave
the right-hand lane.

• • •

No one laughs at your favorite jokes anymore.

Comfort takes the place of fashion.

You're not a kid anymore when . . .

Someone breaks wind and you don't laugh.

. . .

You take along an umbrella anytime it's cloudy.

. . .

You floss.

The top of your pants is closer to your armpits than to your waist.

You are always cold.

• • •

You dry-clean your blue jeans.

• • •

You plan vacations and stick to the plan.

Someone sees
you naked and
screams.

The shopping mall is your fitness center.

• • •

You need Nikes for balance instead of for jogging.

• • •

All of the pictures on your walls are framed.

The neighborhood kids know that if they hit a ball into your yard, they'll never get it back.

DAVID BOYD

You're always asked to say the blessing.

• • •

You wear knee-high stockings with everything.

• • •

You don't dare go out on New Year's Eve.

You are obsessed with
the thermostat.

DAVID BOYD

The elastic is broken in your control-top pantyhose.

• • •

There are no cinderblock and board bookcases in your house.

• • •

Your forehead is twice as long as it used to be.

The spare tire on the back of your RV has your family name and where you're from painted on the cover.

When you talk about "good grass" you're referring to someone's lawn.

• • •

You prefer restaurants where fries are not an option.

• • •

You can still remember when you stayed up all night, you just can't remember why.

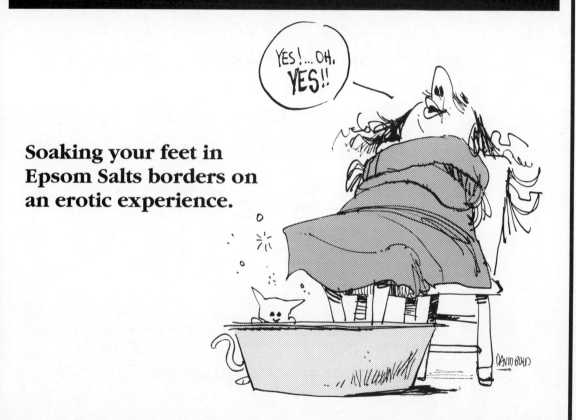

Soaking your feet in
Epsom Salts borders on
an erotic experience.

You're not a kid anymore when . . .

You've seen Halley's Comet . . . twice.

• • •

Strangers ask you to please put on a bra.

• • •

You hope it doesn't snow.

• • •

You add a room to your house to store
unused exercise equipment.

Your ears are
hairier than your
head.

You're not a kid anymore when . . .

You get into a heated debate about
pension plans.

• • •

You can't sit still without falling asleep.

• • •

A skateboard is not a transportation option.

The size of your
trouser waist
depends on how
low you wear them.

You're not a kid anymore when . . .

People see your high school picture and laugh.

• • •

Your wife has more hair on her legs
than you do.

• • •

You start believing that you really did walk five
miles to school barefoot and in the snow.

Your snoring is legendary.

You're not a kid anymore when . . .

You finally realize you don't get
something for nothing.

• • •

You put your dirty clothes in a hamper.

• • •

You don't understand MTV.

Nobody wants to see your cleavage.

You're not embarrassed to be seen in
public with your parents.

• • •

You have more than 30 photos of relatives
displayed in your home.

• • •

You look forward to taking a bath.

You're not a kid anymore when . . .

**You finally realize that
alcohol doesn't agree with everyone.**

Your idea of the perfect nightcap is Metamuscil.

● ● ●

You can go bowling without drinking.

● ● ●

You find no humor in bladder control jokes.

Everyone is tired of hearing how bad your back hurts.

People ask you to knit them a sweater.

• • •

You actually call about the adjustable bed
they sell on T.V.

• • •

You have a bumper sticker that says "I'd rather
be watering my lawn."

If you're seen running, someone should
call the police

• • •

You got cable TV just for the weather channel.

• • •

You get excited about jury duty.